HELP!
MY LAUNCH PLAN SUCKS

By Mal & Jill Cooper

eBook ISBN: 978-1-64365-048-7
Print ISBN: 978-1-64365-047-0

Cover Art by Malorie Cooper
Editing by Jen McDonnell, Bird's Eye Books

TABLE OF CONTENTS

JILL'S JOURNEY INTO MARKETING

I've wanted to be an author ever since I was a little girl. When I was a preteen and other kids were meeting at shopping centers or climbing trees, I was sitting behind my word processor, banging out stories. It helped an awkward and shy kid pass the time and hide from the world, but there was no denying that I loved telling stories more than anything.

And from the very beginning, I knew it was something I wanted to do for the rest of my life.

But life grew busy, and things got in the way. I didn't fall into self-publishing until 2012. By then, I had ditched the Agatha-Christie-style mysteries I wrote as a kid (Still love you, Agatha) and was writing paranormal YA thrillers. Nothing I wrote was written to market. I hopped around from genre to genre, writing whatever struck my fancy.

Which means that at first, I made very little money. This was before 20BooksTo50K, and before there were a slew of indie cover designers and editors. It was the wild west of indie publishing. But I still did it and I still loved it. I hadn't realized then it was possible to make real money from writing books.

It's the dream. And dreams so often seem intangible.

Fast forward to 2013 when I wrote a little time travel thriller called *15 Minutes*. It was the first in the Rewind Agency series, and it was actually popular. It made #1 in the hot releases chart. That was the first time I ever sold more than 100 books in a single day. People started emailing me about the second and third book, and I felt a hint of what might be possible.

It probably would've hit even bigger if I'd realized what I had on my hands at the time. I had picked up some momentum, but I still wasn't thinking like a serious businesswoman. Not until everything started to gel into this new concept about advertising on Facebook, rapid releases, branding your covers instead of just picking what you think is pretty. I hung out in forums, and learned everything I could until I was giving other people advice. Until I was coming up with concepts for covers based on colors and typography and branding.

Then I decided to start advertising Mal's books (under her M. D. Cooper pen name) while she was off working the daily grind as a computer programmer (You know the old story, working too many hours, spending 60+ a week away from home).

I started with *Outsystem* way back in 2015. The book was three years old at that point, but no one had really discovered it yet. The first month after running a low-spend ad, the book made $800.

Ads were easier to get back then. So we sparked up a bunch of them, and when Mal's third book came out, things just exploded.

And the rest is history.

I figure, if I, a chronic genre-hopper and genre-smasher, can figure all this stuff out, anyone can. But I'm here to tell you not to make the mistakes I did. Think as a businessperson, not a hobbyist. It is possible to write books you love and write for marketability. It is possible to even write a genre mashup, if you sell it right.

And that's everything you need to think of before you launch a book or series. Where does it sit? What genre does it fit into? Are the tropes right? Does my cover look like it belongs with the list of bestsellers on a given genre list? Because if it doesn't, it won't sell as well. But if it hits the key demographic, you have a much better shot.

And if you have all those boxes checked, then you're ready to plan an epic launch.

Jill Cooper

WHAT MAL'S LEARNED ABOUT LAUNCHING

As Jill outlined above, she (and later I) learned a lot about book launching and marketing in 2016 and 2017, when we were really getting our careers going.

But in 2018, I was releasing so many books (nearly one a week) that the number of launch tasks I was doing had dropped to only the bare essentials. Luckily, the raw momentum one gains from releasing that many books brings its own launch excitement, and I rode the wave until January 2019.

At that point, I had planned a break…a whole six weeks without a release. I was kinda scared, but I needed to take some time for myself and just breathe for a bit.

During that break, I took a look around at other authors and what they manage to sell and earn, as well as the tactics they use. I found that there were a lot of authors earning income close to ours while producing a fraction of the books we did.

I feel like I should take a moment here to highlight that with my Aeon 14 universe, I'm doing something different than what a lot of authors are seeking to achieve. I want to tell the largest single science fiction story of all time. I plan to eventually have 500 books written in this universe, and, quite frankly, that's going to take a herculean effort for a decade or two.

My uber-rapid-release schedule has more to do with that than making a ton of money; however, I do have a few things I need to do.

One of them is still love what I'm doing. Releasing a book a week forever and always feeling like one's under the gun is not a great way to enjoy life. I was burning out. I wanted to learn how to keep up a good pace, one that I could sustain for the foreseeable future, while also making enough from this career to keep doing it full-time.

I needed to learn to work smarter, not harder.

So I took a longer look at the authors who release 2-4 books a year and earn similar incomes to Jill and I (in the $500k to $1MM range), and saw that they were making much better use of certain tools than we were.

Things from stretching out the teasing of new content, to using Goodreads to drive sales (Right? That's crazy), to a host of other tactics. Many of them I knew, but I just wasn't doing them.

Jill and I talked about how we should make a spreadsheet of each task for each launch so we wouldn't forget stuff. That idea evolved and changed until it turned into this book and its accompanying worksheets.

Okay, enough of all my blathering, let's dig in!

Malorie Cooper

WHAT WILL THIS LAUNCH PLAN BOOK DO?

This launch plan book will help you figure out what type of launch works best for your personality type, writing methods, living situation, and schedule.

There's not going to be a lot of filler or too many anecdotes. It'll be the nitty gritty of what you need to know so you can go on and plan your empire.

Not everyone has tons of time to dedicate to planning, writing, and launching. If you work full-time, have small kids, or just have dozens of commitments, you need to maximize your time and pick a plan that works best for you.

I know all about that. I launched quite a few books with a toddler, and later a preschooler, tugging at my yoga pants. Some days, it was all I could do to write a few thousand words during naptime before crashing in the evening. That was my reality at the time.

You'll have to ask yourself—and be *honest*—what can I realistically do with the time I have?

Your sanity will thank you if set realistic goals and realistic expectations.

A good plan will help set for you target dates for a successful launch, no matter the type of strategy you select. Spreadsheets, worksheets...we have it all to help you plan and organize the best release you can possibly have!

We're going to assume a few things moving forward, and trust that you have done your homework.

Jill and Mal assume you have...

- A well-written and well-edited book. It should be a finished product—or it will be at the time of release.

- A professionally designed cover that fits your book's genre and market, fitting in with the top-ranked books in your genre.

- A blurb that is on point! It sells, it describes, it has a call to action. It makes other writers jealous because it's such a deliciously perfect blurb. If you're iffy about blurbs, you can seek out blurb services. However, we think it's best for an author to take a stab at writing their own blurb first, because no one knows or loves your story like you do.

- Willingness to do the work.

TERMS OF THE TRADE

Yes, boring, but necessary. I want to get a few of these terms defined and out of the way, so that when we get into the meat and potatoes, you'll know what they mean.

MAILING LIST

A subscription-based email list for readers. This is key to marketing to readers on your own terms; sales, new releases, author news, freebie short stories. Really, how you use it is up to you, but ideally, sign-up should be open to all, and you may want to segregate organic signups from ones you get via targeted activities (such as multi-author giveaways).

READER MAGNET

A reader's magnet is something to attract readers to your mailing list so they'll sign up. A short story, a deleted scene, a novella, all set in your anchor universe.

DRIP CAMPAIGN, ONBOARDING SEQUENCE, AUTOMATION

You may see these terms mentioned from time to time in the book, and you may have heard authors use them in the past. Generally speaking, these terms are interchangeable.

13

They describe an automated sequence of emails that are sent out after a new subscriber joins your list. Typically, the sequence begins with a thank you email, which is followed by information about your books, and eventually emails that pitch and sell your work.

BOOKFUNNEL AND STORY ORIGIN

BookFunnel and Story Origin are places you can upload your reader magnet stories in order to deliver them to readers' devices. In return, you'll get the reader's email address to import into your newsletter.

READER FUNNEL

Any time there are sales, there is a sales funnel. This is the number of steps it takes to get a customer (in our case, a reader) from first awareness of us as authors, down to the final sale.

Ideally, your funnel should have as few steps as you can get away with. More complex products require longer funnels, but that typically doesn't apply to books.

PROMO SITES

These are sites where you pay to be featured in their newsletter. Readers sign up to get emails from them about book sales and deals for specific genres. Examples of these are BookBub, Robin Reads, Book Barbarian, etc.

NEWSLETTER SWAP

A newsletter swap is when you contact authors in your genre in order for them to feature your book and/or sale in their newsletter. In turn, you feature their book in your newsletter at some point. Usually, your book is not the only other title they'll have in their newsletter, and you're not expected to send out a newsletter just about their book, either.

PRODUCT PAGE

Though we usually talk about selling on Amazon, this applies to all vendors. The product page is the "sell page" for your book; if there is a button that starts the process of taking someone's money in exchange for your book, that's the product page. For most of us, this will be our book's listing page on Amazon.

A SOLID FOUNDATION

Even if you've already written the book, don't skip this section—especially if this is your first launch. Despite having a lot of launches and titles under your belt, you may still want to skim through, as there might be some nuggets tucked in the pages.

A good launch involves a lot of interconnected pieces, and at the end of the day, requires a book that is poised to sell. Knowing who your book is written for, and aiming both it and all your marketing efforts squarely at the right audience is crucial to a good launch.

In a perfect world, this will have been on your mind as you planned and crafted the book. You thought about the main character, the book's setting, and the story arc with the reader in mind. If it wasn't, you're going to need to figure out what type of reader is most interested in your book before you launch it.

If you lay the groundwork at the beginning of the process, it'll take the pain out of the entire experience, and make all your efforts pay greater dividends.

Let's dive in and paint a clearer picture of what we're talking about.

BRANDING: YOUR BOOK'S IDENTITY

Branding encompasses everything from the presentation of your series and cover design to font choices and layout. To really get a leg up in the market, you'll want to explore the top selling books in your genre and study their covers *and* interiors.

Really study them and see what colors they use, what types of fonts are in use, and what images are popular. You're not doing this to copy the competition's cover, but to make sure your cover fits in.

You want to stand out, but you don't want to stick out. This isn't the time to say you don't like romance covers with a man chest on the front if you're writing steamy romance novels.

Remember, your book cover isn't for you. It is for the readership you want to attract.

So swallow down everything that says you want to be groundbreaking, unique, and unusual, and remember it's okay to fit in. You want to remove all potential barriers between your book and the reader clicking "Buy".

Readers browse for books that fit a mold they already have in mind. When they see your book, you want them to think, "I am going to love this book" because your cover and branding sells them on exactly what they want.

From there, you can go and pick your fonts and hire a really good cover designer who has experience in your selected genre.

BUT WAIT! MY GENRE IS A MASHUP

Many new authors (and a few seasoned ones) will look at their book and think of the ways that it bends genre and brilliantly blends a bunch of tropes together.

The urge will strike you to try to market your book to everyone, and to put elements reflecting all the things on the cover and in the blurb.

I've (Mal here) fallen prey to this as well. But it is very, very hard to market a mashup to people. They're not sure if the book knows what it's doing, or if it will have enough of the tropes they like between the covers.

So pick the main thing your book is about. My books cover lots and lots of topics, but I typically market them as Space Opera or Military Science Fiction. I do this because I can really drive home how the books will satisfy those readers, and it helps me focus my message.

So, hard as it may be, pick one genre and one central element (a trope, if you will) and put that front and center in your branding and marketing.

TITLES AND SERIES NAMES

Every genre and sub-genre is filled with buzzwords and phrases that will sell more books. Getting these into your title or series name will help a lot.

The reason for this is twofold. The first is related to how search functionality is used on websites. When a user comes to Amazon (or any other retailer), they usually search for the product they want rather than browse through lists.

Amazon builds a metadata listing for each book in their search system, and that listing has a hierarchy of importance when it comes to the items that describe your book. While we don't know the exact details, it is clear that the title, subtitle, series name, and the two main categories you pick play a big part in your book's search result placement.

That means if you can put keywords and phrases commonly used in your genre into your title, subtitle, or series name, you're going to have a leg up.

Look inside ↓

Outsystem: A Military Science Fiction Space Opera Epic (Aeon 14: The Intrepid Saga Book 1) Kindle Edition

by M. D. Cooper ⌄ (Author)

★★★★☆ ⌄   345 ratings

Book 1 of 3 in Aeon 14: The Intrepid Saga

(Malorie's Outsytem book title on Amazon)

FINDING THAT TITLE AND SERIES NAME

First, you must identify what sub-genre your book is going to fall into. That's a bit outside the scope of this book, but there are a lot of books that cover the topic. Once you have your genre picked, you need to study the market and decide which buzzwords will be best for your series.

A great way one can do this is by combing through bestseller listings. There are also some excellent tools out there you can use, such as Kindle Spy and KDP Rocket (now called Publisher Rocket).

These tools can aid you in finding the top keywords used in your genre. Don't stuff every keyword you find into the title and series name—they should still make sense. But do your best to choose terms users are searching for on Amazon.

An additional method is to simply start typing keyword ideas into the Amazon search bar and use the auto complete dropdown to help clue you in on what is popular.

If you really want to dig deep and find out what is popular in terms of genre, trends, subcategories, and keywords, consider getting a K-lytics report on the genres that interest you. The monthly recaps on what is popular can be career-changing. You can buy the reports that just interest you, or subscribe to their monthly program.

We always use K-lytics before launching a new pen name in a new genre. K-lytics will show you popular trends emerging, and hot niche markets. We can't recommend them enough!

LET'S TALK ABOUT YOUR EMAILS...

Okay, we're harping on this a bit, but it's really important. Your newsletter is your direct line to your readers, and a good newsletter takes a long time to build up, so don't wait to start yours.

At this point, you should have established your series branding and have some awesome titles and series names ready to go. Your next step is to get this information to your readers.

What's the most cost-effective way? (I bet you can guess what we're going to say.)

Other than a Facebook page or a fan page—where, let's face it, people don't see your posts unless you pay for boosts—your newsletter is the least expensive way to get your message to readers who are genuinely interested in what you have to offer.

Because building a newsletter takes time, this needs to be one of your first tasks—especially if you're a new author or launching a new pen name). You need to start this a few months, at the very least, before launch. During that time, you need to engage your subscribers. If you have other books, you can talk about them, but if you're just starting, let people get to know you a bit. Your life, your motivations, what you love to read, and what made you want to write.

At the beginning, they are still relatively "cold". You don't know them. They don't know you. You want to warm them up! You do that by asking engaging questions, sharing photos of your pets, and giving them a small piece of you.

BUILD A BETTER MAGNET

You might be asking how one generates a
mailing list with no books and no content.
We're here to help!

You might be asking how to grow a newsletter if you don't have any content. The first step would be to write a reader magnet. A reader magnet is something freely offered in order to hook potential readers. You can use sites like BookFunnel or Story Origin to deliver this story to new readers, and capture their email address for your mailing list.

Ideally, one should be thinking about your reader magnet before you write your series, though it's usually possible to retrofit one into your storyline. We like to have them planned out before starting a new series so it's easier to make sure the series universe supports a solid magnet that both stands alone and feeds into the book/series you want to market.

Our reader magnets are typically between 10,000 and 15,000 words. We don't skimp on editing and a cover; this is your first impression, you want it to be good. You're going to have this magnet front and center for a while, so it needs to hold up to scrutiny and show off your skills.

Don't put your reader magnet up on Amazon (or any other
retailer). You want the only way to get this magnet to be
signing up for your newsletter.

Once you have the magnet story set up on BookFunnel, you can join their group promotions for free. Also join Facebook author groups for your genre. Then keep an eye out for promotions in those groups.

No one thing will make or break a successful launch (other than not having the book done), but if there is one thing that can really boost your success at a low cost, it's your newsletter. Not only by the promotion of your books in it, but in the ability to swap with other people.

A dozen newsletter swaps can put your book in front of as many as a hundred thousand readers. That's a huge number, and well worth the effort—especially considering that you can do it again and again and again.

EXAMPLES OF READER MAGNETS

After I (Jill) wrote my YA time travel thriller *15 Minutes*, I released a top-secret document from the time travel agency featured in my book. This was my initial magnet. Later, when I had more time, I wrote a 6,000-word short story leading directly up to the events of the first novel.

It was written from the main character's (Lara Crane) POV, and featured the same punchy suspense style that I used for the full novel.

In my sweet romance series, I wrote a 15,000-word short story about a waitress falling for a billionaire. It's super sweet, set in the same small town just a few decades earlier, in the 1950s. But the characters from that story show up as great-grandparents in the full series.

That also allowed me to bring back local businesses, just with new owners. Readers email me all the time about how much they love this story and the reminiscent angle it adds. I love it too; it's actually one of the best I've written!

I don't even mind that I gave it away for free because it did its job. Thanks to a great cover and blurb, I was able to grow a 1,700-person mailing list in about three weeks, and right on time for launch.

Mal's books (and the Sci-Fi I write with her) frequently feature close-knit teams of people that tackle adventure and danger. We have a number of magnets for those books, all built around the backstory behind how the team first got together. These are always designed to add depth to the main story, and give readers some "aha!" moments no matter which order they read them in.

MAGNET RECAP

- It should be set in your flagship universe.

- It should take place before your first book, but it can be about different characters. Or the same ones.

- The tone should be the same so that if they like the reader magnet, they'll also like your book series.

- This may be the first time that readers have ever heard of you, so make sure the magnet is polished, edited, and proofread. Treat it with the same care as you would a novel.

WHAT IF I HATE TO PLAN?

Uh-oh! Full stop!

Plans...schedules...I hear you.

Early in my career, they made me break out in hives! (Jill here, I don't think Mal has ever broken into hives.) Back when I was writing my YA paranormal books, I was a busy mom to a very young child. I never knew when I'd find time to write, or how long it would take to finish a book. Just thinking of setting a deadline would bring on the hives.

I don't like hives, ya'll.

So I didn't set dates or make plans. The book was done when it was done. And by that time, I'd just release it because I was so eager to get it out there.

Sure, I booked book blog tours (remember those?) and did some Facebook launch parties, back when they were marginally effective. Maybe I'd send out a newsletter, and sometimes I'd get out advance reader review copies on time. Then I'd sit back and wonder why the book didn't sell that many copies and why it didn't have any reviews.

If you've been at this for a while, then I bet you've done this, too. It's okay to admit it, this is a judgment-free zone.

If none of that resonates, or maybe you haven't released yet and are reading this book to avoid making those mistakes, then you've got a leg up.

For the rest of us who have a string of half-baked releases somewhere in our past, there is a path out. The beauty of indie publishing is that it's never too late to have a successful book series! Not only that, even if you release a book and it barely moves any copies, you can launch a promo once the series is complete that can breathe new life into those sales! Mal and I have done that several times.

More on that later.

For now, let's work on the current problem: you need to *commit*. Too bad that's not a four-letter word. It kind of sounds like one.

The Writing Speed & Lifestyle Survey (which you can fill out now, or a bit later) is going to be your friend and help you determine how long it'll take you to finish writing a book. Please make sure it's realistic. Don't say you are going to write 5,000 words a day if you really can't. You'll be stressed out, unhappy, and feel down on yourself because you've set yourself up for failure.

Take stock of your day-to-day life and figure out your average available writing time. If you can squeak in an extra ten minutes here or there, all the better.

If you don't know how much you can write in a week without your life imploding, take a few weeks to write as much as you can, and document what you can do. Take your average and not your high. Life happens!

Let's say you know you want to write a 63,000-word book because that's the sweet spot for your genre. You know you write about 2,000 words a day on Monday, Saturday, and Sunday. This gives you 6,000 words a week without modifying your existing schedule. At that pace, you'll be done with your first draft in a little over 10 weeks.

Set that as your target draft end date. Chances are that you'll need two weeks to a month in order to finish the 2nd draft. Be conservative and set dates you know you can hit. Mark that as the date you want to schedule your editor.

We'll say that again.

Schedule your editor in advance...as in, before you have finished the book. Yes, you can do it, and moreover, it'll motivate you to finish on time. While you're at it, reach out to your cover artist and get them in the pipeline (if you haven't already).

The availability of your cover artist and editor are a big part of when you can release your book.

Once you have dates from them, you'll be ready to start filling in your launch plan on one of the appropriate worksheets (linked in their respective chapters and at the end of this book).

If you're able to write *more* than 6,000 words a week, then you can afford to be more aggressive with your dates—though don't get too carried away. Pad them a bit. You might get sick, or something might come up. Parents falling ill. Kids off from school. Maybe your creative process needs periodic chill days, when you just eat popcorn and watch movies. Mental health is so important, you guys!

How much you decide to pad it is up to you. But do pad it. You'll thank yourself later!

You're not ready to set up your launch yet, but we're close. Let's look at some questions we need solid answers to.

- First off is the date your editor will have the book back in your hands.

- Estimate how long it'll take you to go through edits. If you've never done it before, give yourself one to two weeks (the first week usually involves crying and refusing to look at the edits).

- Get a date your cover will be done, and make sure there's time for revisions and a full print wrap.

- Once you have that target date, decide whether you want to send the book to a proofreader, or if you're going to send it to ARC readers right away. I like to give ARC readers 2 weeks to read a book (That's Jill's timeline, Mal gives her poor readers just a few days).

Now you have enough information to work backwards and know how long the entire production process for your book will take. We can start filling in dates and putting together a plan.

Working backwards:

1. Release Date

2. ARC Readers & Proofing

3. Review of edits

4. Editing

5. Second Draft & Revisions

6. Writing the book

Looks easy, right?

We firmly believe that you don't need to write super-fast or kill yourself pulling off a rapid-release in order to have a successful launch. What you need is a thorough plan. Smooth and consistent production is better than writing and publishing in bursts. A steady pace will ensure you don't burn out or ignore yourself, and still have time for a social life.

Just like with anyone else, personal relationships are healthy and really important for writers. I know, who would have thought that having a life beyond the keyboard can be great?! It's possible to be a writer with healthy habits. You and your writing can both thrive.

If you're new to launching and planning a release, fill out the Writing Speed & Lifestyle Survey. Think about word counts and some solid target dates for milestone goals.

KNOW YOUR BUDGET

Writing, producing, publishing, and marketing a book takes money. Easily a few thousand dollars to do it well.

Because of that, it's not hard to blow through your budget if your dollars aren't allocated in advance—or you forget a crucial step. Here's a handy dandy worksheet to help you understand the costs, and determine both how much you need to spend and what is feasible.

Figuring out your launch budget will play a part in determining which type of launch you can afford. Don't be dismayed if you want to go big and can't. You can always take profits from one launch and put it toward another one. There are ways of making even soft launches really work for you.

We have a simple budgeting sheet on our supplemental page, you can grab it here.

PREORDERS & RANK

Preorders are a contentious topic—one that cannot be discussed without first talking about sales rank...which is also a tricky subject.

WHAT DOES A GOOD RANK DO?

When speaking of sales rank, we're talking primarily about it in context of Amazon. It used to be that a good rank could almost magically drive sales in a self-sustaining way, but that is much harder to achieve now, and typically takes a huge spend to hit the high numbers where Amazon readily promotes your book for you.

However, getting a #1 spot in a category (be it overall or in new releases for that category) gets you the orange tag of goodness next to your book's title on the product page.

Something to keep firmly in mind when selling books is that you're selling them to *people*. Certain things will encourage people to buy a book. High among these is social proof.

Social proof is anything indicating that other living, breathing human beings thought that something was good. We've become inured to machines pushing products at us to the point where we just don't trust a lot of recommendations anymore. But we still trust the opinions of other people.

And that's where that little orange tag comes into play.

The tag, be it a #1 Best Seller or #1 New Release, in a given category tells readers that a critical mass of other people has liked the book enough to buy it. That, along with reviews, is the best way outside of price to convey the value your book has.

And since that orange tag is driven by rank, that is one of the main reasons to seek a high one.

WHAT DRIVES RANK?

Your book's sales rank is quite simply how many sales it has had over the past 30 days, give or take a few. Amazon doesn't tell us how it is calculated, and the formula has clearly changed in the past. Sales in the last 24 hours count more toward your rank than sales made 30 days ago.

"Borrows" count just as much as sales. A borrow is when a Kindle Unlimited reader downloads your book. Also, it doesn't matter what price your book is at, a sale is a sale is a sale when it comes to rank (and remember, in this case, a borrow counts as a sale).

That number is stacked up against every other book on Amazon, and then whichever has the most sales gets the #1 spot, and every other book follows after in order.

That's something important to keep in mind. Your number of sales and borrows can stay perfectly steady, but your rank can go up or down depending on what other books are doing.

So sales and borrows drive rank, and we want rank to get the orange tag of power.

PROS AND CONS OF PREORDERS

Here's your first con: preorder sales count at the time the reader makes the order. Which means (because your book's rank only reflects sales in the past 30 days) if you have a 90-day preorder, any 'sale' you make in the first 60 days won't be reflected in your rank when release day comes.

The next thing can be both a pro or a con, depending on the size of your readership. One of the things Amazon cares about is your book's sales history. Books that consistently sell well will be more likely to end up in recommendation emails and closer to the top of search results.

If you have a long preorder and no readership buying the book, then you're training Amazon that your book doesn't sell. However, if you have a long preorder and enough readers to gobble up 10-20 preorders a day, then Amazon will have a very different opinion of your title.

Again, that rank you're trying to get is mainly for the orange tag, the social proof that your book is good. Other than that (and the back-patting you can do), the rank doesn't serve any significant purpose.

So in this case, the question is will your preorder cannibalize your rank to the point where you won't be able to get the orange tag upon release?

Keep in mind that Kindle Unlimited borrows count toward rank, and readers can't borrow until release. Mal has more than enough readers to do +90-day preorders on books and still get an orange tag on release just from KU borrows alone, but not everyone does.

If you're just starting out, or going wide (not in KU), then it's advisable to keep your preorder short.

Something that is a definite pro to preorders is that you get the reader's purchase early on and don't have to hunt them down again later.

This is more useful after the first book in a series. At the end of the book (if you did your job well), the reader is on an emotional high and very likely to buy the next book. A link to purchase the next in the series right after "The End" is compelling, and captures that reader for the next installment.

Now you don't have to worry about finding those readers with an email, ad, or social media post later on. Amazon will magically deliver the book to them on release day!

ADDED BONUS FOR PREORDERS

If you've been at this for a while, you may have found that sometimes when you put up a book, it can take hours or even *days* to get approved and made available in all regions.

Nothing messes up a launch plan like the book not being live on Amazon.

Because of this, we advise always doing a short preorder (the shortest you can do is four days). This guarantees that the book will launch at the right time, give you a few days to get your series updated on Amazon (if there are other books already out in the series), and also get your print and ebook linked before release.

THE FINAL WORD ON PREORDERS

Just kidding, there is no final word. But here are a few guidelines.

YOU MIGHT WANT TO DO A SHORT (1-4 WEEK) PREORDER IF:

- You have 200 – 300 Kindle Unlimited readers, and your book is in a category where it's easy to get a #1 New Release tag. To make this determination, check the rank of the book with the #1 New Release spot in your easier categories. If it's over 20,000, then it should be something you can reach with around 200 KU borrows.

- You want to have a guaranteed release date and not worry about the book being in limbo for a few days.

- You want to have time to link the print and ebook versions.

- The book is in a series and you want to ensure the series list is updated.

- It is the first book in a series and you really want to aim for a #1 Bestseller Tag.

YOU MIGHT WANT TO DO A LONGER (4-12 WEEK) PREORDER IF:

- This is a later book in a series.

- You have a huge readership and you want to capture the sales as early as possible.

- You have such a large marketing machine that you aren't worried about rank and orange tags.

Notice there's no suggestion to *not* do a preorder at all? It just makes sense to get the launch timing certainty that a preorder gives you, and those four days won't hurt if you don't let anyone know that the book is out (for those of you worried about diluting release-day rank).

FIND YOUR PRICE

It's time to duke it out—I mean talk—over how to price your release. This is a hotly contested debate that rivals whether or not pineapple belongs on pizza.

PREORDER PRICE

I strongly recommend against doing a 99c preorder, and here is why.

1. Some KU readers will decide to grab the preorder at the discounted price. That costs you rank and money upon launch.

2. People buying during preorder are likely top fans who want to support you. Run your preorder at full price, and then do a sale afterward (communicating clearly that you are doing this).

3. Running your preorder at full price will allow you to do a KCD (Kindle Countdown Deal) two days after launch and make 2x the royalties on your launch sale.

PRICE AT LAUNCH

If you have a preorder, the "launch price" we're discussing here is what you set the price to the day your book comes out—if you change it at all.

Do you launch at full price or 99 cents? Either can be the correct answer, depending on what it is you are trying to accomplish. You can utilize both but in different situations:

99 cents will garner you more purchases and more impulse buys.

Full price will get you more money.

Take a look at your genre and see what the people at the top of the charts are doing. If your genre has a lot of niche markets, look for authors and books similar to your own. For example, if you write cozy mystery cat sleuth books, and everyone launches at 99 cents, that may very well be the way to go.

Another thing to consider is that if you're a brand-new author, launching at 99 cents will get more eyeballs on your book. However, not everyone who buys a 99-cent book reads it. There's a perceived value of a 99-cent book; some people treat it like a throwaway item. If you price at $2.99 or higher, more people will read the book because they value that money more.

Of course, if 500 people buy your 99-cent book, yet only 60% of them read it, you might not mind if those people go on to preorder Book 2 and beyond.

In addition, launching at $2.99 or greater gives you more wiggle room to run promotions later. If your book is permanently 99 cents, your only option after that is to discount it to free. It's the only real deal you can honestly offer at that point.

I think free has its place, but we don't like to do it too often or too soon. We'd like that book to fly as high as it can for as long as it can before dropping it to Free. At the very least, we'd like to have three books out in the series first.

You also make more money if you launch at full price:

- At 99 cents, if you sell 200 copies, you'll only make around $70.

- At $2.99, if you sell 100 copies, you've made about $200.

If you're really hustling to get those sales, then a higher price is less work for more money. It depends what your goal is for this specific launch.

- If your goal is to get as many new readers as possible, pricing at 99 cents makes sense. The greater sales volume can give you a great sale history with Amazon. However, launching at 99 cents is not a guarantee of becoming 'sticky'.

- If you want to make as much money as you can, pricing to market for your chosen genre is a solid strategy. In addition, if you're a brand-new author, or have a brand-new pen name, getting some early reviews is going to be *extremely* important if you decide to price this way.

There are also ways to make use of both strategies for the same book during your launch cycle. Having a 99-cent sale is still a solid and very important tactic.

- Launch at full price ($2.99 – $6.99 depending on your genre, but don't price yourself out of the game. Make sure you do your research.) This also include the preorder period. There's nothing nicer than a big wad of cash on release day!

- Plan a 99-cent sale for 1 – 2 weeks after launch. Book a few promotional newsletters, plan your ads, and get some newsletter swaps with authors in your genre. If you're consistent with your schedule, your superfans won't get upset that you've run a sale right after release.

You can even give your readers advance notice in your newsletter that you will be running a sale in a week, but they can choose to purchase it at full price if they don't want to wait. This tactic works really well for us. Most of the superfans are happy to buy the book at full price. Some will even buy it when it's on sale, even if they previously read it in KU.

LIMITED RUN EDITION LAUNCH

There are times you'll want to launch at 99 cents regardless of other considerations. Here are a few thigns that work well.

- Limited run editions that allow you re-package existing content and build hype around an exclusive sale.

- Boxsets that are priced to hit the sweet spot of a low-cost purchase while also sure to get you more KU reads (if you're not wide). Remember, if the titles contained in a boxset are wide, the combined set cannot be in KU unless you remove the other books from the wide retailers.

- A short 3-month KU term can be useful in situations like this if you do it right.

When launching a limited run boxset or other special edition, you'll need a solid plan and an intense marketing push:

- Great cover that looks good and hits the appropriate tropes.

- An off-the-hook blurb and enticing sale copy that will suck people in.

- Hit your newsletter and ARC team and ask them if they have previously reviewed any of the books in the boxset. If so, encourage them to review the boxset as well. Starting off with even a small set of reviews will help you when booking paid promotions, and will help readers make an informed decision.

- Don't skimp on the AMS and Facebook Ads.

- Line up a good number (10+) of newsletter swaps.

You'll treat it like its own launch even though all the content has already been made available in different editions. Be prepared to really put in the work for one of these launches. Also remember that making a boxset is something to do when a series is at the end of its life and is beginning to fade.

Readers of boxsets like boxsets. They might have never seen your series before.

It's also a great chance to use a different cover strategy and hit a new demographic. If you write women's fiction and have had women on the cover, now is a great chance to try a beachy landscape or a picturesque house and attract readers seeking a different aesthetic.

KCD SALES

A Kindle Countdown Deal (KCD) is something you can do if you're enrolled in KDP Select (Kindle Unlimited). For five days every three months, you can choose to have a 99-cent deal and receive 70% royalties.

- It's only in the U.S. and the UK (and you'll need to set them up separately).

- After the KCD is over, you cannot change the price on your book for two weeks. So plan carefully.

- Your book has to have been available for sale for thirty days (preorder terms count). So this is a great way to utilize a preorder term to your advantage. You can setup a KCD sale as soon as the book is released after the preorder period.

As long as your sale was not a KCD, you can ride the momentum. If the book is selling really well at 99 cents, keep it there. Run your ads, and maybe increase the ad spend if you can afford it and your read through is high.

Keep an eye on the sales and your book rank. As it starts to drop (but before it drops too far), you can raise the price and hope to capitalize on those extra eyeballs who are seeing your book because it's higher on the charts than usual.

- After a Free deal, raise the price to 99 cents. Change your ad to reflect this (or kill the ad and start a new one). Then book a few more promotions and newsletter swaps for the 99-cent period.

- If your book is normally $3.99 or $4.99, set it to $2.99 for a while after a deal. You can launch a newsletter and ad promotion using it as a *'Last chance! Get it on sale while the getting is good!'*

These tactics might help you keep the momentum running a little bit longer so you can gain more followers, earn a little more money, and hopefully find some more superfans.

SELECT A STRATEGY FOR YOUR YEAR-LONG MISSION

No book lives in a vacuum, so before we talk about how you plan to launch an individual title, it's important to have an understanding of your overall strategy... or to craft said strategy, if one is not already in place.

Remember, the number one thing you're doing as an author is earning readers' trust. That might seem a bit odd, but hear me out. The price people pay for a book—three or four dollars—is a pittance, not enough money for the average person to worry over. Even at minimum wage, it's less than an hour's work for multiple hours of entertainment.

A decent trade... if the story is good.

And that is what you need to keep in mind. You're really selling a reader on being able to keep them entertained for 6-12 hours. More than anything, they want to know that those hours will be time well spent, because there is no getting them back.

Again, it's about trust. And a great way to build trust is through clear communication and consistency.

Too many authors take a "When it's done" approach with books, and while a big part of trust is built on releasing quality material, you also need to release it when you say you will.

To have a book both done well *and* delivered when you say it will come out, you need to have a plan. That plan can't be made without knowing how fast you can write and how long it takes you to produce a book. Without knowing that—and understanding where to build buffers into your schedule—you can't plan out the next year of writing and releases. And if you don't have a year or so planned out, it's very hard to come up with a release strategy— which in turn makes your individual launches less powerful than they can be.

So let's suss that out before we go any further.

If you know how long it takes you to write a novel, revise it, review edits, format the darn thing, and publish it, then you can *maybe* skip doing the worksheet. But it might be a good idea to fill it out anyway so you can be sure you're taking everything into consideration.

This sheet will give you a conservative estimate for how long it will take to write a book, and how many you can write a year.

Keep these things in mind as you work on the sheet:

- The time it *really* takes to revise a book. Some authors can revise one book while writing a second, while others can't mix editing and writing. If you are just starting out, you can try it, but don't plan on being able to do it. Even Mal can't edit and write on the same day (though sometimes she tries).

- The time it will take to go over your editor's comments and notes. Don't forget that you might need to get substantial changes re-edited.

- The time it will take to plan a launch and execute the steps. Launching isn't rocket science, but it does take time and forethought. Coordinating with authors for newsletter swaps and just checking to make sure your ducks are in a row will consume many hours of time.

Taking those things into consideration, if I were an author who could write a book in two months, I would plan to release a book every three months. If I'm feeling conservative, or have things like family vacations in the mix, I might up that to once every four months. The beauty of being in charge of your own destiny is knowing you can change something if it is not working for you, but you should also plan for success, so you can feel good about getting those wins under your belt.

Conversely, once you've got a few launches in your rearview mirror, things will get easier and you can take on more without taxing yourself as much. You never know; if you start off by committing to three books a year, maybe by the second quarter, you'll feel comfortable enough to add a fourth book.

Okay, here you go! Dig into the survey and see what you learn about your production potential:

OK... now complete the Writing Speed & Lifestyle Survey Spreadsheet

As someone who has released 44 books in one year (Mal speaking), I don't really recommend going over two books a month. So far as I'm concerned, 24 books is the maximum a sane person can do in a twelve-month period.

Once you fill out the sheet and have a handle on the number of books you can write each year, you can then pick the release strategy that works best for your goals and pace. Let's work our way up from the lower end of the spectrum.

But before we do, remember that this is not a competition. This is about figuring out the right number of books for you to sustainably release each year without risking burnout (or at least, to lessen the risk).

STRATEGY #1: STEADY AS SHE GOES

I can't help but picture Scotty saying "Steady as she goes..." to Captain Kirk every time I see this... we're such nerds.

This strategy is ideal for folks who can write between one and four novels a year, though it can work for higher output authors as well. The idea with this strategy is to evenly space the releases (as much as life allows), and make the most of marketing each stage of your novel's creation and production, leveraging them as touch points and conversation pieces with your readers.

Hallmarks of this strategy include:

- Consistent releases anywhere from 1 – 4 books a year

- Good use of BookFunnel or Story Origin with reader magnets, and a healthy newsletter subscription base.

- Newsletter swaps with authors in your genre. Often 6 – 12 per release

- A progressive series of teaser and promotional images as the book is being produced (covered more later).

- Your focus is to maximize each action you take in the writing and production of your novel; talk to your readers about your characters, why you've made them, what they're doing, etc.... You can feature cover reveals, tease ARC feedback, the works.

- Depending on your budget, you may not pump a lot of money into ads upon release. In that case, write the next book. You're playing the long game.

These are actionable activities that are easy to manage if your life does not give you time to simultaneously focus on both writing and marketing. This sort of strategy often features a lower budget (though that can ramp up as you have more money to spend on launches). Take time to review the example **Slow and Steady Launch Plans** at the end of this chapter to help you see what yours can look like.

If you can, create a release schedule for the entire year. Remember what you learned from the Writing Speed and Lifestyle Survey.

In addition, remember the option to make boxsets and special editions. If you have long gaps in your Slow and Steady strategy, these can help fill the spaces, as well as give you conversation topics with your fans.

CAVEATS WITH THIS STRATEGY

When you're going slow and steady with a year-long release plan, it's important to remain focused. Genre-hopping and writing with more than one pen name will make it a lot harder to build an audience and hold their attention.

Pick a genre and stick with it. Repeat that phrase aloud. "I'll pick a genre and stick with it." Do this for at least one year. Don't hop around. Don't abandon one series to jump onto a new one. It's important to show readers you are dedicated and that you finish what you start. Readers want a complete story. If you abandon a series after book two, they aren't going to be happy. They will lose trust in you, and remember, it's all about reader trust.

That will kill your career faster than anything else.

And if you do hop genres, you should probably consider a pen name....

Uh oh...time for a segue...

USE AMAZON TO SELL YOURSELF AND YOUR BRAND

Okay... that little comment about pen names is a huge can of worms. Heck, we could probably write a book on the pros and cons of multiple pen names.

Aside from keeping in mind the effort required to maintain multiple social media and marketing presences for more than one pen name, you have to keep in mind how your books appear to readers on Amazon.

Every author name on Amazon has an author page associated with it. There, you can have photos, videos, links to blogs, and (of course) a listing of all your books. Readers can also choose to follow you, and if they do, Amazon will email them when new books of yours come out (provided the people who follow you tend to buy).

This is all tied to your pen name and author page.

Having multiple pen names is absolutely necessary in some cases, and can be avoided in others. There are some obvious scenarios, such as if you write children's books and erotica. One certainly does not want those covers mixing on your author page.

Even a genre hop such as hard science fiction to sweet romance likely requires a different pen name, as part of what your author page is doing is convincing readers that you will give them the experience they want. If your page looks like a mishmash, it won't inspire confidence in that.

There are other scenarios where you may not need a different pen name. An example could be a jump from cyber/tech thrillers to more action thrillers. Your readers could very likely follow you if your covers and blurbs show them that they'll get what they like from you, just in a different setting.

Also keep in mind how Amazon promotes you. When you have a new release, they email a subset of your followers. If enough of that subset clicks and buys, they email more and more and more. But if you have cross-genre books, and most of your list is interested in genre A, and your recent release is genre B, chances are that Amazon will never email your full list, and you've just lost out on a significant marketing tool.

When it comes to making this pen name decision, size matters. If you have a large readership and have built up trust with your readers, it's more likely that they will follow you across genres. If you are new and/or have a small readership, it is less likely that they'll follow you.

To put it in perspective, if I (Mal) were to write an Epic Fantasy book, I think that a good number of my readers would pick it up. Most of them are at the point where they're "reading for the author". However, if I had done that in early 2017, all it would have done is told my readers that I hop around and can't focus.

I love that the following segue inside of a segue is from Jill not me. I'm not sure who's rubbed off on who...

Speaking of Amazon, take time in crafting a really great Author Bio. If you write historical romances, your author bio should be radically different than someone who writes gritty thrillers. Your bio isn't just selling yourself but it is also selling your author brand. Read a few bios from the bestselling authors in your genre. See how they craft them. Take a few stabs at it, share it with friends, and see what they think.

You don't need to be overly witty or ironic or even funny. Talk about yourself and your love of the genre you write. Throw in a few tidbits about what makes you personable and relatable. Oh, and mention your pets. For real, guys.

DO NOT COMPARE YOURSELVES TO OTHERS

This is a big one, especially if you're a slow and steady author. Don't compare yourself to other authors' successes stories you see posted online or hear in talks, etc.... Your journey isn't their journey.

Their living situation, work situation, health, everything is all different than yours. You need to work at a pace you can enjoy that also keeps you loving the art of storytelling.

Often, those authors who have meteoric rises release rapidly, which means it's easier for them to snag readership. It is harder for readers to forget an author who is constantly releasing new books.

However, the chances of author burnout are much higher (speaking from experience here). Eventually, something has to give. This isn't a judgment, it's just the truth. Authors cannot churn out words and books forever without eventually needing a break.

You also don't know what is going on behind the scenes—what the author did to get there, how much money they are spending on ads, what their return on investment (ROI) is. Just like everything else online, you only see what they want you to see.

Pace yourself. Worry about only yourself. Consider your known performance to be your baseline, and build on your success month by month, book by book.

In the end, that's all that really matters.

WHAT IS RAPID RELEASE?

Before we can talk about strategies 2 and 3, we need to discuss rapid release and why it's a thing.

Rapid release is a scenario where you write several books in advance (usually 3 – 4), and release one every 2 – 3 weeks. The original rationale behind the 2 – 3 week timing has more to do with the Amazon ranking algorithms than anything else.

The idea is that since there is a cliff after about 21 days or so (simply due to the math behind how Amazon calculates rank), having a new book come out *before* your prior book falls off the rank cliff will bolster both the prior book in the series and your author rank. This will aid in keeping your content visible on Amazon, and your books in readers' minds.

While we often rapid release, we do it more as a marketing technique with readers in mind rather than rank. We also have the ability to keep the flow of books coming and not have a long drought after the rapid release.

Not everyone can do that (be it just your writing speed, or life situation), so you need to be cognizant of your personal situation before diving into a heavy release schedule.

STRATEGY #2: BURST MODE

If you're able to write 5 – 12 books a year, then you can utilize strategic bursts to build momentum.

Rather than just discussing the rapid release of 3-4 books, we want to talk about the entire strategy surrounding that short period, not just a 2 – 3 month period where one does the rapid release and then wonders, "Now what?"

Keep in mind that it's important to have consistency with your readers. If you release four books over two months, and then they have to wait a year to see another burst from you, they might not stick around. You have to keep things moving with steady content after the burst.

At the higher end of this spectrum (8 – 12 books a year), you can do a release burst and still have a good number of titles to follow up with throughout the year, but at the lower end of (5 titles), you may want to keep your burst down to only 2 – 3 books over a 2-month period, with the other two titles coming 3 – 4 months apart.

An advantage to holding the first few books and releasing them in a burst is that often you can write a series from start to finish—or almost finish—before book 1 comes out. There are some significant pros and cons to this method, as well as some serious questions to consider.

Burst Mode Pros:

- You construct the full series' story arc all at once. Book 1 will not have released when you decide you need to change something in book 2 that affects book 1. This gives you the flexibility to play with your world and get the story just the way you like it.

- You can get all the covers and editors lined up way in advance.

- You know when you release, if your book is well written and the cover is branded to market, that you will be able to have a nice Amazon tail from book 1 to book 2, and then move on to book 3.

- You'll have lots of time to plan and organize everything in advance.

Burst Mode Cons:

- If it takes you a month to write one book, you're talking 3 months before you finish the series. And if it takes you 2 months to finish a book, you're looking at 6-7 months before you start to see any real money from the work you're putting in.

- If you're writing and holding for a burst mode release, you're writing about the same world, the same characters for a long time. You could get fatigued or lose focus. You'll have to think up creative ways to keep your drive going.

The big question you need to ask yourself is what happens once you finish releasing this series?

Can you write a new book 1 and 2 before the third book is released so you can keep up your series momentum? Can you be writing a book 4 and 5 in time to capitalize on your success from the rapid release of the series?

You're going to want to think very carefully about whether or not you can maintain momentum before you decide if Burst Mode is a good choice for you. You want to see if it fits your lifestyle, how long you can reasonably go without a major release, and if your attention span will let you get away with writing a complete series back to back with no breaks.

STRATEGY #3: POWER BUILDUP

In a way, this is a combination of Steady as She Goes and Burst Mode. It lets you write in a steady fashion with the ability to burst if needed. It also serves the goal of consistency. It is ideal for a writer who can produce 10-16 books a year, though it can work with fewer—but at fewer than 10 a year, the strategies begin to look more like Steady as She Goes.

The big difference between this and Steady as She Goes is that you don't do the full set of launch activities with every release. You will do a big launch for every 3rd book or so, saving your marketing energy for points where it will yield the biggest reward.

When I (Jill) launched my sweet romance pen name, I knew what month I wanted to launch. I also knew I wanted to build up a stable of books—enough to release monthly for four months—before the first book came out. With a planned release date of book 1 in October, that meant I needed to be writing book 4 when book 1 came out.

Mostly, I did this in preparation for the following year's summer, when I tend to write less so that I can spend more time with our daughter and go on vacation.

It also meant I was utilizing preorders to keep up momentum from month to month in order to build on those releases.

In this scenario, I was working on about 3 books at once.

- Drafting book 3.

- Revising book 2.

- Waiting to get edits back on book 1, followed by reviewing those edits.

- Once book 1 is finalized, that's when I'd format it, upload it and get the paperback version up for sale.

- And then move on to book 4....

Power Buildup Pros:

- I never feel particularly under the gun to finish a sweet romance. If I have a bad day and can't hit my target word count, it's not going to break my schedule completely.

- I have time to really think and plan each book.

- Peace of mind.

- Money can be more consistent in this method than if you are employing a burst mode strategy. For me, it was one book a month. I know many authors who put out more than that, but for me, this was as rapid as I could get with that pen name.

Power Buildup Cons:

- If you're new or just starting out, it can seem daunting to have so many balls in the air at once. Sometimes, if I'm having a bad day, it can even get to me.

- You might feel like a factory line or like you are churning the books out.

- It can be expensive getting all those edits and covers lined up before you've really started to see any money come in, which is something it shares with Burst Mode.

For me, I feel like this is a great release strategy for balancing career and peace of mind. I've struggled with serious burnout a few times over the years. This is the best way I have found to avoid it. When I can feel it coming on, I'm able to slow down more and step back without fearing everything is going to completely fall apart.

Feel free to experiment with these first three strategies, maybe come up with a way that is unique to you. Find what works, and stick with it until it stops working. Then find something else.

Now it's time to talk about the sort of madness Mal revels in.

STRATEGY #4: ONE WITH THE MAELSTROM

This sounds kinda terrible, like a form of writing purgatory where you just spew words out of your fingers forever. As someone who has done it (Mal speaking here), I can tell you that it takes near-perfect conditions to pull this strategy off, and it is difficult to maintain.

In 2018, I released 44 books in a sort of rapid release process where I had a book out almost every single week. Only in one instance were there three books sequentially released in the same series. Mostly, I hopped between series, writing nine separate ones at the same time.

To put it mildly, this is not for the neophyte, and even seasoned pros balk at the idea of a book a week for weeks on end. I do know a few new authors who jumped straight into this, and I applaud them! Somehow, their heads don't explode—though I know few who didn't eventually burn out.

At its slowest pace, this process creates a veritable stream of books coming out every 2-4 weeks. If the books sell, then Amazon will promote your works more, knowing that putting them in emails causes people to click through to their site. Consider that if you go this route, you will constantly be writing, editing, releasing, and then doing it again at least once a month.

An advantage to this strategy is that it minimizes the marketing activities you need to do. There is no need to do cover reveals, or talk up plot points or characters in the months between releases. Instead, almost all of your reader outreach will be about the next book, sales, and the general breathless excitement of so many books coming at once!

Whew!

This strategy has its own cons (other than burnout, which *will* happen at some point).

Reader fatigue is a real concern. It could be that readers in your genre don't read a book a month (other than the whale readers), or that they want more variety than a single series is giving them—which is one of the reasons Mal does different series at the same time.

You might also lose ARC readers, if they have commitments to other authors that they have been ignoring to keep up with you.

You'll need to find a balance, one where you aren't seeing diminishing returns from releasing too fast. This is genre dependent, and doesn't have a tried and true number, but if you find yourself putting out books faster and faster with smaller and smaller income from each release, it might be a good time to take a hard look at your strategy, and determine whether it's helping or hurting.

When following either this strategy or the Power Buildup strategy, your biggest struggle will be focus. There will be a lot going on all the time: edits coming in, proof and ARC feedback, covers, newsletter swaps. You name it, the distraction will be beating down your door.

It's important to work smarter, not harder. Seek out help and utilize it where you can.

- Hire a VA to help you with your launches and ARCs. Get them to update your Facebook page with release information, and seek out newsletter swaps in author groups.

- Hire a housekeeper to clean your house twice a month. Trust us, it's life-changing!

- Carpool with other parents to earn yourself a little more time in the mornings. Trade off with your spouse. That's 30+ minutes of writing you can add a few times a week!

- Understand it isn't just you who is a part of this launch, but your whole family. Get them involved with meal prep, cleaning, and everything else that goes along with the day-to-day.

Remember, if you want this to be a career and not a hobby, you have to treat it like it's your job. Respect the efforts you're putting in, just as you would if you were paying for college to get a better day job, or burning the midnight oil at the office to advance your career.

If you hone your writing skill, make efficient use of your time, and launch your books deliberately, then *this* can be your sole income.

THE PLANS

With the general strategies out of the way, let's talk plans.

PLAN #1: IMPULSE SPEED

This first plan is the sort you employ with the Steady as She Goes strategy. It has the most marketing touchpoints with a goal of maintaining reader engagement between releases, and then making the most of each release because it has to carry you for several months.

You're also not putting a ton of money behind the marketing, leveraging less expensive avenues as you build up your coffers over time.

With this plan, we don't recommend going with longer pre-orders, as you don't want to dilute your release; nor do you want to train Amazon to believe your book doesn't sell. Remember, sales history is important.

What you'll need to determine in advance:

- A target release date

- When your cover artist can deliver the cover

- Your editor's availability and speed

- Proofing time

- Formatting and publication time

- Time for ARC reviews

There are two ways of establishing these dates. One is to set a release date and work backward, and the other is to determine all the necessary timeframes and work forward to your release date.

We recommend working backward from release to a starting date because it is a more honest way of doing it, rather than trying to cram in everything you need to do in a fixed timeframe.

We have two spreadsheets you can use to work out these timeframes: the preorder and the non-preorder versions. In addition, if spreadsheets are not your thing, you can fill out our PDF worksheet to go through all the things your launch will require, and establish your dates (link at the end of the chapter).

Note: The spreadsheets don't have dates for every single marketing activity you'll need to do. An entire email campaign with all of its touchpoints could be an entire sheet on its own.

Ideally, this launch is going to take place over the course of about ninety days, maybe more. You'll want to start just talking with your readers about the setting, or maybe the main character. Ask them questions over the first month or two, and then roughly a month from release, you should do a cover reveal.

If you are doing a preorder, don't reveal the cover till the preorder is up. That way, people can take immediate action and preorder the book.

Whether you have it on preorder or not, you should also have the book up on Goodreads, and encourage people (especially KU readers) to have it on their bookshelf, as Goodreads will send them a release notification, and will also show your book to more people as a suggestion if it is on a lot of bookshelves.

As the release date is coming up, share your blurb, talk more about the characters and their motivations. If you plan to run a sale shortly after launch, let your readers know that, as they will appreciate your honesty.

You'll also want to work hard to have a lot of ARC reviews in place for launch, which means you should try to have the print edition up first (and linked to the ebook) so that people can put their reviews on it. That will give you a big Day One boost.

Post-launch will be your newsletter swaps, but likely not paid promotions. Try to get at least 6-10 swaps.

Remember, because this plan is typically paired with the Steady as She Goes strategy, you want to communicate a lot, but also keep things short and to the point.

Grab the Spreadsheet and PDF from our

supplemental documents page:

thewritingwives.com/launch-plan-worksheets.

PLAN #2: WARP FACTOR ONE

While it is fundamentally the same as the Impulse Speed plan, Warp Factor One is more intense. It requires more thought and planning, as well as more capital for advertisements and booking paid promos. It takes the basic foundations from the Impulse Speed plan and ramps them up.

It typically takes place over a shorter period of time, which is why you're leveraging things like paid promotions, more swaps, and existing newsletter activity to signal boost during the ramp-up.

As with the Impulse Speed plan, your big items are:

- A target release date

- When your cover artist can deliver the cover

- Your editor's availability and speed

- Proofing time

- Formatting and publication time

- Time for ARC reviews

You'll also need:

- Two to four promotional images

- A reader magnet on BookFunnel or Story Origin. Ideally, it should be up and running before you start book 1. But at the latest, before you finish *writing* book 1.

- You'll need to have grown and warmed your newsletter subscribers. Rather than talk about this release over a longer period of time, this plan assumes that you've been doing other releases/activities, and have been sending at least one newsletter a month to keep your readers engaged. Share photos, ask questions, ask their advice, make them feel like you're their friend and not just selling to them.

- 8-10 newsletter swaps with other authors in your genre.

- Send ARCs (10-20 to start) 2-3 weeks before the book releases. Make sure you follow up to keep them engaged. I send reminders one week out, three days out, on release day, and then a week later. Make sure to be polite and thank them for their time!

- Post to your Facebook page or profile with cover reveals, excerpts, reviews. (One week out, at least one post a day. Max two times a day. You don't want to slam them with information too fast or start to wear out your welcome.

- Run a Facebook ad 1-2 days before release. Minimum of $5-10 dollars a day.

It certainly is a lot to think about all at once. The best way to tackle each of these tasks is to give them milestone dates so you know when to take care of them.

Grab the Spreadsheet and PDF from our supplemental documents page: thewritingwives.com/launch-plan-worksheets.

PLAN #3: STAR GATE

This is the biggest and most involved of the plans. It's the perfect strategy for book 1, or maybe that series ender (whether it's book 3 or book 6). This plan takes everything we've talked about before, builds on it, and maximizes everything. So if you were getting your skills up on Impulse Speed as well as Warp Factor One, now it's time to take what you've learned and push it to the limit.

As with the other plans, you'll need to determine:

- A target release date

- When your cover artist can deliver the cover

- Your editor's availability and speed

- Proofing time

- Formatting and publication time

- Time for ARC reviews

You'll also need:

- 4-6 promotional images. Some of these might be text on an image, a header, a series of headers, launch countdown, etc.

- A reader magnet on BookFunnel or Story Origin. Ideally, it should be up and running before you start book 1. But at the latest, before you finish writing book 1.

- A well-warmed newsletter. This means you send at least one newsletter a month, and you talk to your readers. Share photos, ask questions, ask their advice, make them feel like you're their friend and not just selling to them.

- 10-25 newsletter swaps. Spread your newsletter shares out so you're never featuring more than 2-3 other authors in your NL a week.

- Send ARCs (20-50 if you can) 2-3 weeks before the book releases. Make sure you follow up to keep them engaged. I send reminders one week out, three days out, on release day, and then a week later. Make sure to be polite and thank them for their time!

- Post to your Facebook page or profile with cover reveals, excerpts, reviews, early reader feedback, your inspirations on the setting, characters, or themes and story ideas. One week out, at least one post a day. Max, maybe four times a day (if you have more than 1000 likes). You don't want to slam them with information too fast or start to wear out your welcome.

- Guest post on other authors' Facebook pages, ask authors in groups you're in to social share (nicely, not spammily). If you have friends who write in the same genre as you do, this is a great time to ask them to help you out. Always offer to mention them in return, we're all in this together!

- Start a Facebook ad one week before release. $5 dollars a day to start. Ramp up each day, once you're comfortable with the CPC.

Check out the worksheet to help you organize your thoughts and plans for this galaxy hopping release! It's bigger than the others, so give yourself more time to plan it and organize it. This is a great time to utilize a VA to help you out, once you have a plan built.

In an upcoming section, I'll talk about how to find a VA, and what to look for to get a rock star who will be able to help your launch be a success!

Just like in the previous sections, you'll want to figure out how long it'll take you to write this book (or series) realistically, without killing yourself or driving your family (too) insane. Yes, sometimes you will make sacrifices, but let them be on your own terms. If your publishing schedule is too aggressive, you may begin to feel like you're failing, and that's not something anyone wants to feel.

Set realistic and reasonable goals for your life. Not the goals of your BFF writer, or someone you've heard speak. Everyone's production ability is different, but it doesn't mean it won't change as time goes on.

What we're saying is, if you haven't yet taken the Writing Speed and Lifestyle Survey, now's the time!

Grab the Spreadsheet and PDF from our supplemental documents page: thewritingwives.com/launch-plan-worksheets.

REMEMBER: BE FLEXIBLE

We just talked about scheduling all sorts of dates, but you also want to be flexible within that plan. If something you tried isn't working, drop it. If life gets in the way and you know early on that plan needs to be modified, do it as soon as you can.

If your spouse goes out of town and you're able to get more writing done in the evening, do it! Release dates are great targets, but if you're able to get a book done in advance, it's a no-brainer to go whole hog and get it wrapped up. Your future self will thank you!

Personally (Jill speaking), I can really crank out the words during the school year, but the summer is my slow-down period. I love the beach, and I love spending time with my daughter; that means in the summer, I don't get as much written.

And that's okay.

It really is okay.

Give yourself permission to enjoy life. It'll help you avoid burnout.

I should note that I do need to write a little in the summer to maintain my sanity, but I won't stress myself out, because my daughter is around more at that time, and I need to 'mom' more than I do during the fall.

Not only that, but the break helps me recharge!

PRE-LAUNCH MARKETING STRATEGIES

Many of these strategies will serve you well after launch, but you'll want to kick them off well before the book comes out. We'll start it off with some free (or mostly free) ideas to help you build an audience.

FACEBOOK LIVE

Facebook loves video, and will show that format more often than text and image posts. However, you might be nervous about doing a video. After all, we're authors—we don't really like to put ourselves out there. We'd rather let words and books do that.

Unless you're Mal, but she's not exactly normal in that regard.

Even so, it's worth exploring, and is good practice for in-person pitches. Speaking of practice, do some dry-runs recording yourself to see if you have any tics to deal with, and get your delivery honed.

It's okay to admit you're nervous. I get nervous! Mal does too, though it's hard to tell with her!

The videos you'll want to make can be anything from your book's cover reveal (with book in hand, if possible), to reading an excerpt or the blurb. You can also talk about your inspiration for the book, or announce a sale and/or the release date.

Acknowledge the people who are watching, and try to involve them and what they are saying into your video. It can range from 5 – 10 minutes, but try to be concise and not go on for too long. Once you're done, the video will be available for replay for people who didn't catch it live.

If you can do one a week until launch, great. If you can only stomach doing it once, that's fine too. At least now you've ripped off the band-aid!

CONTESTS

Contests used to be really popular, and though they don't seem to be as prevalent, they still work! It's not necessary to give away a Kindle or anything expensive if you can't afford it. Prizes can be knickknacks that fit your book's theme, or books that are in the same genre as yours. Often, you can get authors to donate copies, or you can buy them yourself.

Just don't give away the current book you are releasing and promoting, otherwise the contest can cannibalize sales.

Rafflecopter is an excellent tool you can use to run and organize your contest. It prompts people to (and tracks whether they):

- Like/Join your Facebook fan page and group

- Sign up for your newsletter

- Follow you on Amazon or BookBub

- Read a short excerpt, and answer a question found in the text

- Post or tweet, and share in other ways as well.

Make sure you have plenty of freebie ways to enter your contest. (By Facebook Terms of Service, you can't make liking your page mandatory, but you can make visiting it mandatory. It has to be up to the user if they decide to like the page or not.)

Also, if you want to have an option for buying or ordering your book, make sure it's not the only method of contest entry. By U.S. law, you can't make a purchase mandatory for entering a contest.

And never, ever, ask people to review your book as a contest entry. Amazon will smack you, or ban you, if you get caught.

Other than that, share your contest on Facebook, and ask your fans and street team (or ARC team) to enter and share the contest for you! Make sure you hit your newsletter about that as well.

If you want to widen your reach, you can start a multi-author contest, but you'll need to add ways to enter the contest that benefit those authors as well, which may dilute your results. Be sure to weigh that return against the cost and group marketing power.

BUILDING YOUR NEWSLETTER AND LAUNCH EXCITEMENT

You've been getting eyeballs on your BookFunnel/Story Origin reader magnet via free marketing strategies. Now is a great time to throw a low spend ad on Facebook, and try to grab as many email addresses as you can.

At $5 a day, this ad was getting me roughly 27 – 35 new email addresses a day. When my (Jill) book finally launched, my brand-new pen name had a newsletter list with 950 addresses on it, and I did everything I could to maximize my use of it.

Once you have those addresses, they are yours until they unsubscribe. So I made sure to send regular emails without overwhelming them. I did things such as:

- A welcome with an excerpt/blurb from book 1.

- An excited message talking about my release coming in one week, along with a picture of my cat, Ms. Fudge Swirl.

- More excerpts around day three before release.

- And finally, the big release email.

In each email, you want to be warm and authentic. You want to talk about yourself, ask the reader questions to which they can respond, and always include the link to your upcoming book. If you're including other authors' books in your newsletter, or a BookFunnel/Story Origin promotion link, put it after all of your big, important stuff.

We think it's great to periodically send a one-off newsletter that exclusively highlights another author and book that you just *know* your list is going to love; don't do it too often, and not on your regular newsletter day. For example, if you always send your newsletter on a Sunday, send this one-off email on a Wednesday, or some date well-separated from your regular day.

Now that you're collecting email addresses like a champ, also remember to include the BookFunnel/Story Origin link in the backmatter of your books. Some people will find your book organically online and purchase it, and won't have come across the link to get your reader magnet. You want to give those people a chance to read your freebie, and also capture their email address for your list.

At this point, your reader magnet is mostly self-sufficient. Check in on the ad every few days and make sure it's still bringing in those email addresses. If the CPC is low and the email collection is high, I would consider throwing more money at it. But only if you're comfortable doing so.

I usually cap at it $10, just because I don't want to spend more than that a day on collecting email addresses. What you decide to do is up to you. Which is a good time to talk about....

Data! To maximize your tracking of folks who sign up for your reader magnet, be sure to use your Facebook Pixel on BookFunnel/Story Origin. Instructions on how to do this are in our Facebook Ads book.

ADVANCED REVIEWS (ARC)

First things first, you want to make sure your book has been edited (even if not proofread) before you send out any ARC copies, but you can start building your ARC team a month or so before your first ARC is out. Any closer, and it might be hard to find members. Any further, they'll start to forget about you before you send the file.

Places to find them:

- Your newsletter is the best place to start. If you've built your list off of BookFunnel, these readers love a free book, and may already love to review. I copy them into a special ARC reader mailing list.

- Ask your fan group, put a call out on your page, and on your personal Facebook page as well.

- Booksprout. I haven't got a huge amount of ARC readers this way, but I have gotten one or two.

- There are services that will find readers and send your ARC copies out for you. Some of them are expensive, and I don't have any personal experience with them. Just know they are out there. **Note: You're not paying them for the reviews. You are paying them to find the readers and email the book files out. It is still compliant with Amazon's TOS, and the number of reviews you will receive (including their content) is not guaranteed.

Once your ARC reader list is built (at least 10-20 people to start is great), and it's about three weeks out from release day, you should send your first message, which may or may not include the book file. Mine goes something like:

> *Thank you for joining my ARC team! My book is written for Sweet Romance Book Lovers! You'll receive the book next week, and I am super excited for it to finally be in your hands. I would love reviews to be published on this date.*
>
> *Your help is really appreciated,*
>
> *Humble Author*

If you want the reviews to be posted before the release date on Amazon, you can publish the print book at this point, and make sure the ebook and the print book are linked together. This does mean your print book is available for purchase, but most people won't opt for that format.

Also, don't publish a print book more than 30 days before the ebook, or BookBub will no longer send the New Release Alert for your followers.

ARC REVIEW GATHERING PROCESS

About two weeks before book release, I start sending the BookFunnel links for ARCs so it will be available for readers as a .MOBI and a .EPUB file. The accompanying email is a little longer, but I find it helps to set expectations of the ARC reader:

> *Thank you so much for agreeing to review Sweet Romance Book Lovers! Here is a link to download the book. It has not*

been proofread, so please keep that in mind. If you find a typo and would like to send it to me, feel free! If you do, I'll make sure to thank you in the foreword of the book.

When you post your review, it doesn't have to be long. Just what you thought and why. Please don't post spoilers, because we want to ensure that everyone has a GREAT reading experience.

Make sure your review is HONEST. If for some reason you think the book is worth 3 stars or less, I still invite you to post your review! But I humbly ask that you wait until after XYZ date to ensure a solid book launch.

Thank you for reading!

Humble Author

With that email sent off, I will then follow up with an email one week later, and then again on release day. One week after release, I send a quick thank you email:

Thank you so much for all your reviews! The book is doing great, and that in part is thanks to you. If you haven't posted your review yet, there is still time. For those of you who are caught up, the next ARC for review will be sent in one month's time.

Thanks for your help!

Humble Author

This email will most likely ensure you get a few more reviews, and maybe even an apology for being late. Be gracious and understanding. Life happens and, after all, ARC readers are pretty much doing us a service for free, even if they are getting a free book in the process.

NEWSLETTER SWAPS

Newsletter swaps really make a difference in an effective launch when it comes to reaching new readers!

The concept is pretty simple: you find authors in your genre who will post about your book and sale in their newsletter. Then you return the favor.

When posting another author's book in your newsletter, you should:

- Include the cover.

- List the sale price.

- Add a tantalizing bit of information about the book.

All authors would probably agree that it is best to have your newsletter content first, and then include the authors you are swapping with after that.

There are a few services that help with newsletter swaps, such as Author-XP. In most cases, your best bet is to post about it in Facebook groups. Some author groups allow it, even if only on certain days of the week. It's best to always adhere to the group's rules when trying to organize a promotional thread such as this one.

You can also search for 'Newsletter Swap' or 'NL Swap' in the Facebook search bar. There are a few genre-specific ones that I know of for SF/F and Sweet Romance. If you comb around, you should be able to find some good ones that fit your needs!

AUTHOR FOLLOWING

Other than your Facebook page and newsletter, there are a few places readers can follow you and receive new release alerts:

- Amazon. Granted, sometimes their new release alerts come out way after the book does, but it still doesn't hurt.

- Goodreads. Goodreads is great when it comes to notifying your readers of new releases. Encourage your readers to follow you there, as well as add your books to their shelves.

- BookBub. They will email your followers about a new release as long as it's new content—so no boxsets—and a full-length novel over 150 pages.

- Booksprout. This service is still new, but it is building a following.

When it comes to Amazon and Bookbub, you can find writer services that will launch giveaways for readers if they follow a specific group of authors on Amazon and BookBub. They cost money to join, but usually not much. And it can really be worth the effort.

THE RELAUNCH

You spent a lot of time planning and launching your individual books, so why would you want to go through and do it again?

Mostly time and money.

If you spent a year (or 5 years) writing and releasing your series, people who were reading it at the beginning might have forgotten about it. With so many authors jumping into self-publishing, this can happen easily, even if your craft is seriously on point. A relaunch (even a soft relaunch) is all about reminding them they loved your work. Plus, it's an opportunity to point out that you have five new books they didn't know about.

As an example, a soft relaunch would include sprucing up your blurbs, but keeping everything else pretty much the same. Then you would organize a big sale to get more eyeballs on your books, and hopefully see a healthy rise in the ranks. In this case, you aren't changing the titles or the covers. It's more of a marketing tactic than a full-on launch.

But you treat it like a launch with:

- Facebook ads, AMS ads, or any platform you feel comfortable with

- Booking some promotions, applying for a BookBub

- Newsletter swaps

- Mobilizing your ARC and reader groups to share about your sale

THE FULL REBRAND

You may decide at some point it's time to rebrand. This could be for a host of reasons, including:

- You just finished writing a long series

- Your covers missed the mark the first time

- Your covers didn't miss the mark, but the market has shifted

- Your series has been out for a few years, and the market has different cover and title tropes you want to hit.

There are a few things to consider when thinking about a rebrand:

- It can be expensive to buy 3-9 new covers at once. So if you're going to do it, make sure you have taken the time to study the current market, including colors, fonts and composition. As you tweak yours, continue to ask yourself 'Would this cover fit in with the books at the top of the genre'? If you can't answer yes, then you need to keep working.

- Think about the current hot keywords in your genre. Make sure you can work a few of those into your title and series name. You don't want it to sound nonsensical, but you should be able to include one or two that the search algo can pick up on. Plus, the words you choose should make the reader think, 'That's a book for me. I love action Sci-Fi!'

You want to take time to plan your rebrand. It's not completely dissimilar to launching a brand new book. You might decide it *is* a brand new book, and even get a new ASIN. You can do this and consider it a second edition if you've:

- Changed, added, or edited the text.

- Changed the cover.

- Changed the title and series name.

You can link it to the old book for a while, and ask Amazon to move the reviews over before unpublishing the previous version. Just make sure you include something in the book description that makes it clear this new book used to be the old book under the previous title. You don't want a lot of angry readers on your hands.

If you do get a new ASIN, you'll have the advantage of hitting the Hot New Release list again, but don't overuse it. Only use it when it makes sense and you really are launching a different version of the product.

In either case, you'll want to hit the launch hard and get everything you can out of it. That means you'll want:

- Fan awareness. Tell them online, and craft a newsletter

- Newsletter swaps

- Well-crafted ads, wherever you are comfortable launching them. Facebook, AMS, and BookBub are good sources.

- Promos. Consider launching at an 'introductory limited time' price.

THE AUTHOR LIFE

To be honest, I went back and forth on whether to add this section to a book about launch plans, but I thought it should at least be discussed.

Let's face it, if you don't take care of yourself and your body, it'll be hard to do everything it is you want to do.

Writing, for most people, means sitting around a lot, and that's not good for your health. So when you're so busy, how do you take care of yourself to ensure a long life and a healthy career?

PRACTICE SELF CARE

A writing career isn't easy. It's hard work. You'll be working a lot on all the various tasks that exist, from writing, to marketing, and everything in between. It's easy to put your head down and just run yourself ragged if you let the work take over.

But you need to take care of yourself. Mind, body, and soul.

Without a healthy body, you can't write successfully. You need your hands and your wrists especially. Your mind and your soul, well, those are the heart of being a writer. You need to take care of you.

Plus, if your health starts to falter, you're not living your best life for yourself and your family or friends. You can't do the things you want to do.

And then, well, what's the point?

If you take care of you, everything will be much easier. So when making your launch plan schedules, consider your health and well-being. Account for some time off, exercise, whatever you've decided to do to take care of you.

I can't stress the importance of this more.

JILL'S STORY

I was a stay-at-home mom. I really focused on what I wanted. I wanted to write, I wanted to make money. I wanted to create worlds. So I did. I got caught up in releasing fast. I took care of my daughter and all the things that go with being a SAHM. We played, I focused on her development, and teaching her right from wrong. When she napped, I'd write. If her dad took her out, I'd write.

I stopped going to the gym. I didn't eat meals unless we were all together. I lived on junk food and coffee—a lot. I let myself suffer, and I gained a lot of weight. If I wasn't writing, I felt panicked about it.

My health was in decline. I couldn't walk through the mall parking lot without losing my breath. My knees and back both hurt. I felt guilty and like a bad parent. I also felt like I had no way out.

I was ashamed of letting myself go so far. I wanted to be healthy. I wanted to make sure I lived a longer life. But I couldn't ask for help because I was embarrassed. I didn't think things would ever change—and I'm still in the middle of becoming the healthy, fit me that I want to be.

So I had to take more time for myself. But it was hard. I knew everyone around me saw the decline, but to admit it to myself was still really tough.

Fast forward a year since I've dedicated myself to being healthier, and I'm down about 4 pant sizes, but I'm still not perfect. I do eat more veggies, fast intermittently, and only eat at scheduled mealtimes.

It's made me healthier. I get sick less. Two summers ago, I was sick for a full month, and the resulting headaches lasted about six months. I haven't had that problem since.

I'm happier. I have more energy. In the long run, that makes my writing easier. And better too.

HAVE A HEALTHY DIET

Eat the color of the rainbow, and I don't mean Skittles! Eat fruits and vegetables. You don't have to adhere to a specific diet, but eat to fuel your body, and stay away from as much junk food as possible.

As a writer on the go, I find intermittent fasting to be a lifesaver on my schedule. I eat dinner, sometimes lunch and dinner if I'm hungry, and it makes meal prep a lot easier when my daughter is in school.

I also try to alter my eating every once in a while, to keep my body in suspense so it doesn't know what's going on. I do it in hopes of keeping my metabolism charged and ready to go.

My daily schedule looks something like this:

6AM – 6:30AM: Groan, get out of bed, drink some electrolytes, some water, and make coffee.

By 8AM, I'm usually drinking coffee with some MCT Oil.

Homemade bone broth during the day. If I'm going to eat lunch, I have it around noon. If not, I eat dinner at 6PM.

After 6PM, the goal is not to eat again.

I fast anywhere from 18-24 hours most days. Some weeks, I might throw in a 36-hour fast, but only if I'm feeling good and energetic. If I start to get cranky, it's time to eat.

It's important to break your fast the right way. The wrong way will send you running to the bathroom! I usually break my fast with low protein, maybe a small amount of a healthy fat, and some veggies.

Another tip to keep you going, especially when fasting, is to drink lots of water. We all know writers love coffee and/or tea, but water is important for your body.

Speaking of....

TAKE CARE OF YOUR BODY

Your wrists and back are important. If you injure your hands, it can be devastating to both your career and lifestyle. So listen to what your body says. Take scheduled breaks throughout the day to rest your hands, go for walks, enjoy the world we live in. Your body and mind will thank you for it.

A desk setup that has your hands low and your monitor at eye-level is key. It takes some getting used to, but over the long term, your body will be a lot better off.

If your wrists are bothering you, you can invest in a quality keyboard or try dictation. Dragon Speaking is the way to go, software-wise.

Some authors swear by dictation, and others loathe it. I'm somewhere in the middle. Like any skill, it takes a while to practice and get into the flow. It can be hard to get the same joy from speaking as from writing, but it might be worth the effort if it saves your hands—and your career!

STEP AWAY

There's always going to be author drama, or Facebook drama, drama anywhere, really. It's important to not get pulled into it. It's never good to gossip, it can really hurt your soul. It also hurts your productivity and your creativity.

So step away.

Don't engage, and don't give in. Just close the window, or do something else. Go outside, live in the moment. When you're out for a walk, or sitting at the beach, online gossip and scandals that felt huge at the moment suddenly melt away.

Getting away and unplugging as much as you can will make you realize how petty and not worth it author drama is. Or any online drama.

SO MUCH TO DO, SO LITTLE TIME

It's easy to get caught up in the stress of having to do it all right now. I'm not immune to this. In fact, I get stressed out a lot. I'm thinking of books and writing, plus providing for my family while also being a constant presence in my daughter's life. I try not to put too much pressure on myself, but it's hard!

I find that meditation is important to my well-being. I practice mindfulness as often as I can to reset my priorities and keep my to-do list from overflowing. There are only so many hours in the day, and I'm not superwoman, as much as I'd like to be. Setting reasonable expectations for the house, my obligations, and my career is a must.

If you find you can't quiet your mind, look into meditation. Here are a few tools I find useful when I'm reeling and need to reset myself fast:

- Online journal

- Online meditation

- Mindfulness ebook

- My fav Youtube meditation

I like to-do lists as much as I hate them. I put the things at the top that I *really* have to do, and everything else falls beneath that.

As a mother and a wife, family often comes first for me. Whether it's a school meeting or making dinner, I try to get my high priority items done as quickly as possible.

It can be hard. Some days, it means I'm working at 6AM rather than tidying up the house, but sometimes these sacrifices are necessary and they are always worth it.

If you find letting go of all the tasks around you, I suggest breaking them into chunks. For example, if I know I need to fold laundry and make dinner before getting back to the word count, I will:

1) Fold laundry for 10 minutes.

2) Go write for 10, 15, 20 minutes. Whatever I can afford to do that day.

3) Then run into the kitchen and prep the veggies by doing the cutting and dicing.

4) Then I'll finish up what wasn't done with the laundry, and start dinner. While that happens, if I haven't met my word count goal for the day, or if there are still admin tasks to do, I'll do them in the kitchen while standing at the counter. Maybe for 20 minutes. Maybe until I finish that scene. Again, it'll change day after day.

Not exciting, but it keeps me moving, and allows me to do what needs to be done.

Other options are to outsource to house cleaners, meal delivery systems, etc. Sometimes when you're super busy, you need to delegate! Don't spend your time doing something you hate if it's going to cut into your productivity time.

Outsource, delegate, find ways to get help. If your family and spouse are supportive, get them on board to help with the house chores too.

MY KID IS SICK, MY CAR BROKE DOWN, AND I WANT TO CRY

Everyone's heard that life is what happens when you're off making plans. It sometimes feels doubly so when you're a writer. You have to know this is going to happen. When it does, the first thing to do is cry.

I think it's healthy to just let out all that emotion so you can feel it, acknowledge it, and then let it go. You can't stop life from happening. You can't stop the bumps in the road, you can only navigate over them as smoothly as possible. It's important to see these as detours, and not something that is going to completely derail you.

You cry, then you come up with an action plan. Remember, a dream is only a wish until you write it down. Make a list, as detailed as possible, as to how you are going to get through whatever crisis life has thrown your way.

If you've made a launch plan, then you know how many days you can realistically spend dealing with your life crisis before you need to move on. If you were smart and padded your schedule a little bit, you have time to catch up.

Get help from family if you need to offload some projects or tasks that block you from writing. Use a grocery delivery service, hire a bi-monthly cleaning service, whatever you have to do to free up some extra time you can devote to getting back on track.

WHAT TO DO WHEN YOUR SELF ESTEEM QUITS

Everything is always great until it isn't. The same can be said for writing. You're doing fine until self-doubt creeps in. That little voice saying you can't do it anymore. You're tired, you want to quit. You think all of the words you're writing are crap. There are dirty dishes in the sink, what the hell are you going to do?

Big questions.

It sounds counterintuitive to take time for yourself when you're already behind the gun, but that is the very first thing you should do. I like to meditate when my mind is spiraling out of control.

I also believe in being grateful, and practicing mindfulness. I believe we attract what we put out, and we can manifest the life we want by visualizing it.

Here are a few of my favorite resources:

- Let Go & Relax 10 Minute Meditation
- Dear Universe: 200 Mini-Meditations
- Good Days Start with Gratitude Journal
- And for those of you that like things a little more badass: Zen as F*ck: A Journal for Practicing the Mindful Art of not Giving a Sh*t

Other things you can do:

- Create a vision board of where you want to be at the end of the year, 5 years, 10 years. Get pumped up for everything you're going to do.

- Have a person. Or maybe two.

I have one person, other than who I am married to, that I run to when times are tough. When I'm crying, overworked, and overwhelmed, she will talk to me and tell me how amazing I am. How I have this in the bag. She says all the right things that I need to hear when I'm spiraling down the sink.

Speaking of sinks, my bathroom totally needs to be cleaned right now. Some days, that's enough to tip me over the edge. Today, not so much, because I am on *fire*. I have this. I know I do, and every day I strive to succeed a little bit more than I did yesterday.

To sell books, to keep climbing the mountain—whether you're just starting, or you've reached a really hard cliff—you need to believe in yourself above all else. If you don't, or if you consistently can't, it's going to be really rough.

So find your person. Be that person's person. Bolster each other up. Writing is a solitary act, but being an author doesn't have to be. We all have felt what you're feeling right now at least once. Maybe a dozen times.

It's a long road. A marathon. And everyone gets tired. Just don't quit.

If that doesn't help, eat some bad food and take a stinking nap.

WORKSHEETS, CHECKLISTS, AND SPREADSHEETS

All of our worksheets, spreadsheets, and supplemental PDFs can be found at:

thewritingwives.com/launch-plan-worksheets

We will keep these sheets up to date with new ideas and information.

To get updates, subscribe to our mailing list:
eepurl.com/gGjqYL
Using print? Take use your phone's camera to follow the link.

NON-FICTION BOOKS BY JILL & MAL

HELP! I'M AN AUTHOR SERIES

Help! My Facebook Ads Suck *Second Edition*
Help! My Launch Plan Sucks

Check out other **Help, I'm an Author!** books coming soon at www.thewritingwives.com/our-books

THANK YOU

Thanks for taking the time to read this book. We really do hope it helps you out on your journey as an author.

As you all know, reviews are the best social proof a book can have, so we would greatly appreciate your review on this one.

The Writing Wives,
Jill & Mal Cooper